Christmas Trivia

Variant without quiz master:

In the version without a quiz master, the reader can also guess because no solutions are marked within the questions.

Further back in the book, there are the same questions, but with marked answers.

Here you will also sometimes find explanations of the correct answer.

And at the end of the book there is an overview of all the correct solutions at a glance.

Have fun solving it :-) !

1   When was Christmas first celebrated?

A) in the 4th century

B) in the 15th century

C) in the year 3 after Christ

2   How many needles does an average (1.70 m tall) Christmas tree have?

A) 470.000

B) 690.000

C) 180.000

3 Who ordered the census that Mary and Joseph traveled to Bethlehem for?

A) Pontius Pilate

B) Emperor Augustus

C) King Herod

4   What day the British call Boxing Day?

A) December 26th

B) December 24th

C) January 6th

5   Where does the term gingerbread come from?

A) Probably the mixture of Laib and Libum

B) A sheet cake cut into pieces

C) Jesus received life on earth

6 What is the name of a legendary Christmas dish from Great Britain?

A) Santa Cheese Boots

B) Jelly Bag Cap Cake

C) Plum pudding

7 Where does the tradition of Christmas bonuses come from that many employees receive?

A) A tradition in Israel

B) From a tradition of the earlier guilds

C) From the toy industry lobby

8 What is the name of the Grinch's dog in "How the Grinch Stole Christmas"?

A) Max

B) Charlie

C) Spike

9 What Christmas beverage is also known as "milk punch"?

A) Eggnog

B) Hot Chocolate

C) Mulled Wine

10 What is traditionally hidden inside a Christmas pudding?

A) A key

B) A coin

C) A candy cane

11   Why do we celebrate Christmas on December 25th?

A) December 25th has been a religious holiday since 336 AD

B) It is the day of Jesus' birth recorded in the Bible

C) Pope Leo III established it in 801

12   What is a nativity play?

A) An old musical instrument

B) A play that is performed at Christmas

C) A Christmas board game for the whole family

13 What is special about Finnish Santa Claus Joulupukki?

A) He has no beard

B) He is married

C) He does not have a red coat but one made of reindeer fur

14 According to the biblical Christmas story, which animals witness the birth of Jesus?

A) Ox and donkey

B) Camels

C) None of these

15 In the song "The Twelve Days of Christmas", what gift is given on the fifth day?

A) Three silver spoons

B) Five golden rings

C) Two turtle doves

16   Who invented the Advent calendar?

A) The Romans around 400 AD

B) A German publisher

C) The Chocolate Industry in the 20th Century

17 When does the Christmas season officially end in Germany?

A) On New Year's Eve

B) On December 27th

C) On January 6th or on Candlemas in early February

18 In some regions of Germany there are Dambedei, Stutenkerl or Grittibänz. What is that?

A) Men made from yeast pastries

B) A carousel with singing

C) A Christmas dwarf who brings the rod to bad children

19 The author of "Lord of the Rings" J. R. R. Tolkien wrote...

A) as a child "Five Little Reindeer"

B) involuntarily the book "Letters from Father Christmas"

C) due to a lost bet the song "Jingle Bells"

20 Who visited Jesus first?

A) The Shepherds

B) The Wise Men of the East

C) King Herod

21 Where does the poinsettia plant come from?

A) From the Mohawk of North America

B) From the Aborigines of Australia

C) From the Aztecs of Mexico

22 In Finland, children run before Christmas from house to house. They dress up as...

A) Elves

B) Reindeer

C) Santa Claus

23 Who distributes the presents in Iceland?

A) The 13 Yule Lads, called Jólasveinar

B) Santa Claus, called Jólasveinn

C) The 21 volcano elves, called Eldfjallálfar

24 Where did the idea for the song "Rudolph The Red Nose Reindeer" come from?

A) From the eighth American President Martin van Buren

B) The idea comes from composer Johnny Marks

C) From a children's coloring book

25   In Catalonia, the nativity scene is...

A) a tapa of plums wrapped in bacon as an offering

B) a Catalan Caganer

C) an ivory sledge

26 What famous ballet is often performed around Christmas?

A) Swan Lake

B) The Nutcracker

C) Sleeping Beauty

27 What country started the tradition of sending Christmas cards?

A) Italy

B) France

C) England

28   Where does the Christkind come from?

A) Martin Luther introduced it in the 16th century

B) It comes from Christmas traditions in Scandinavia

C) It is an invention of Walt Disney

29   What is marzipan made of?

A) Walnuts

B) Dates

C) Almonds

30   According to the Office for Christmas Carols in Graz, approximately how many Christmas carols are there?

A) 30.000

B) 3.000

C) 300

31 What is the origin of the custom to put up a Christmas tree?

A) In Israel, fir trees are exotic lucky charms

B) This comes from pagan cultures or religions

C) It says so in the Bible

32 What is Frosty the Snowman's nose made of?

A) A button

B) A carrot

C) A coal

33 How many candles did the Advent wreath have when it was invented?

A) 23

B) From the beginning there were 4

C) 1; in rare cases 2

34 How many parts of raisins, candied orange peel and candied lemon peel must a raisin stollen contain per 100g of flour?

A) 5g

B) 60g

C) 85g

35 What is the minimum alcohol content of mulled wine in Germany to be called mulled wine?

A) 12%

B) 7%

C) There is no regulation for this

36 The grandfather of Cedric (Little Lord Fauntleroy) is

A) Earl of Essex

B) Earl of Grantham

C) Earl of Dorincort

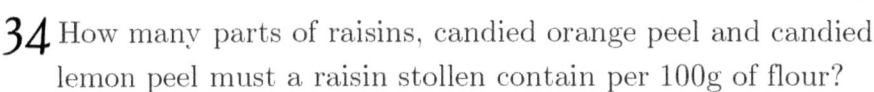

37 According to a survey, what do Germans give away the most?

A) Vouchers

B) Socks

C) Technology

38 What does the Latin word "adventus" mean?

A) Arrival

B) Almighty

C) candle

39 The Christmas Oratorio tells the Christmas story in 6 cantatas. Who composed it?

A) Ludwig van Beethoven

B) Johann Sebastian Bach

C) Richard Wagner

40 What is the name of the miser in "A Christmas Carol" by Charles Dickens?

A) Baltasar Grooge

B) Dagon Drooge

C) Ebenezer Scrooge

41 Which animal do people in Bolivia traditionally bring to Christmas mass?

A) Calf

B) Sheep

C) Rooster

42 What was the Christmas tree originally decorated with before baubles and tinsel were used?

A) Apples, baked goods and paper

B) Gold and silver jewelry

C) Nuts and oranges

43 What do Catholics call the four Sundays of Advent?

A) Matthew, Mark, Luke and John

B) Lithus, Adventus, Domino und Nubes

C) Ad te levavi, Populus Sion, Gaudete und Rorare

44 There is no Santa Claus in Russia, but...

A) Brother Nicolai

B) Father Frost

C) Babuschka Sweater

45 What gifts did the wise men from the East bring for Jesus?

A) Gold, frankincense and myrrh

B) Jewelry, nuts and toys

C) Robes, scrolls and salt

46 What are the two other most popular names for Santa Claus?

A) Santa John and Claus Nicholas

B) Father Christmas and Snowman Nick

C) Kris Kringle and Saint Nick

47 Which spices should definitely not be used in speculaas?

A) Cardamom and cloves

B) Oregano and marjoram

C) Coriander and cinnamon

48 Jesus came to earth to...

A) to heal the sick

B) to take over the government of Israel

C) to save lost people from eternal damnation

49 What was the first song ever broadcast from space?

A) Silent Night

B) Jingle Bells

C) Deck the Halls

50 Where does the Nordmann fir originally come from?

A) Sweden

B) Caucasus

C) Finland

51 What are the names of the other reindeer besides Rudolph?

A) Dasher, Dancer, Prancer, Vixen, Comet, Cupid, Donner, Blitzen

B) Glitter, Snowflake, Glory, Starlet, Cupcake and Brownie

C) Unicorn, Lilly, Arnold, Shooting Star und White Mountain

52 In the movie "Home Alone", where are the McCallisters going on vacation when they leave Kevin behind?

A) Paris

B) London

C) Rome

53 Where do gingerbread cookies originally come from?

A) Israel

B) Egypt

C) France

54 Since when have electric Christmas tree lights been around?

A) 1879, with the invention of the light bulb

B) 1911, a department store chain in Berlin launches it

C) Invented in 1882, used in the White House in 1895

55 What color was Santa Claus' coat, before Coca Cola dressed him in red?

A) Blue

B) Gold

C) White

56 Traditionally, many families in Australia and New Zealand celebrate Christmas on the beach, with...

A) the election of the most beautiful Santa Claus (Mr. Santa)

B) a big barbecue, called BBQ in English

C) a surfing competition on red and white boards

57 What do many people in Poland hang on the Christmas tree?

A) Spiders and spider webs

B) Wool socks

C) Small wooden dolls

58 In which city was Saint Nicholas bishop?

A) Myra

B) Jerusalem

C) Corinthians

59 How many kilos does the average German gain between December 1st and New Year's Day?

A) 1-2

B) 3-5

C) 5-7

60 According to the biblical story, where was Jesus born?

A) Bethlehem

B) Jerusalem

C) Nazareth

61 In the song "Rudolph the Red-Nosed Reindeer", what was Rudolph not allowed to do?

A) Fly Santa's sleigh

B) Go to the North Pole

C) Join in any reindeer games

62 What is the highest-grossing Christmas movie of all time?

A) Elf

B) The Polar Express

C) Home Alone

63 In "The Polar Express", what is the first gift of Christmas?

A) A silver bell from Santa's sleigh

B) A golden ticket

C) A mystery snow globe

64 Which islands do not exist?

A) Advent Islands

B) Christmas Island

C) Easter Island

65 When are the presents distributed in Spain?

A) January 6

B) December 25th

C) February 2nd

66 Where do traditional Christmas pyramids come from?

A) From Mexico

B) From the German Ore Mountains

C) From Kazakh farmers

67 Why is the birth of Jesus something absolutely unique and special?

A) No human being was ever laid in a manger

B) Shepherds worshiped Jesus

C) God himself took human form

68 On which album was the 1986 song "Last Christmas" by Wham! released?

A) Music from The Edge Of Heaven

B) Make it Big

C) Fantastic

69 Has the celebration of Christmas ever been banned?

A) Yes, in Brazil from 1963 to 1971

B) Yes, between 1647 and 1660 in England

C) No

70 Which event takes place every year at Christmas in Rio de Janeiro: Santa Claus...

A) lands in the football stadium with a helicopter

B) gives a speech on Rede Globo, a major TV channel

C) distributes candy to children in need

71 Why is tinsel called tinsel?

A) Llamas in South America were decorated with silver threads

B) The inventor was called Lambrecht Etta

C) It comes from Italian and means metal leaf

72 Continue: And the angel said unto them, "Fear not, for behold, I bring you good tidings...

A) news that will change Israel."

B) of great joy, which shall be to all people."

C) secrets that no one else can hear."

73 What do girls in Sweden traditionally wear at Christmas?

A) Santa Claus coats and fake beards

B) White robes and candles on the head

C) Fur hats and velvet gloves

74 Where is the Christmas story?

A) In the letters of Paul

B) In the Psalms

C) In the Gospels

75 What song did the angels sing?

A) Glory to God in the highest

B) Silent Night, Holy Night

C) Oh, how happy you are

76 What does the X in the abbreviation stand for in English X-mas for Christmas?

A) From the Greek letter Chi

B) This comes from youth language

C) The X stands for the cross on which Christ died

77 Which Asian country is the only one where Christmas is a public holiday?

A) China

B) South Korea

C) Malaysia

78 Which statement is not true? Speculatius...

A) must not contain almonds

B) was initially only illustrated with the story of St. Nicholas

C) is eaten all year round in Indonesia

79   Who showed the wise men the way to Jesus?

A) The Angel

B) King Herod

C) The Star

80   What does the name "Jesus" mean?

A) God saves

B) The Sacrificial One

C) God came as a human

81   What does "Christ" mean?

A) The Anointed One

B) The Savior

C) King

82   How does the Christmas story begin?

A) Once upon a time...

B) And so it is told...

C) And it came to pass in those days...

83   How did the Christmas markets develop?

A) The monks in the monasteries sold their goods

B) Late medieval winter markets for the population

C) It was the idea of clever merchants around 1840

84   What are incense cones made of?

A) Made from resin, charcoal and wood flour

B) From rapeseed oil and gypsum

C) From ground horse hooves

85 What U.S. state was the first to recognize Christmas as an official holiday?

A) Alabama

B) New York

C) Texas

86 The star singers write on the doors C+M+B. What does this mean?

A) Christ, Mary, Bethlehem

B) ChristMas beginns

C) Christus mansionem benedicat (Christ bless this house)

87 Where did Mary, Joseph and Jesus flee?

A) Lebanon

B) Egypt

C) Türkiye

88 Does the Bible say that Jesus was born in a stable?

A) Yes

B) No

C) Instead, the word "shed" is

89 What is myrrh?

A) Beautiful jewelry

B) Children's toys

C) Fragrant resin

90 Why is Jesus often called "Jesus of Nazareth"?

A) He was crucified there

B) It was his earthly surname

C) He spent his childhood there

91 Who was related to Jesus?

A) Peter

B) John the Baptist

C) Luke

92 What does "Merry Christmas" mean in Spanish?

A) Muchas Gracias

B) Feliz Navidad

C) Bienvenidos

93 Why do some people in America hang cucumbers on their Christmas tree?

A) People think cucumbers bring good luck

B) Cucumbers are part of every Christmas meal

C) The smell of cucumbers creates a great atmosphere

94 Which Christmas film features Tom Hanks 6 Characters?

A) Snow Queen

B) Charlie and the Chocolate Factory

C) The Polar Express

95 In which country is Christmas dinner ordered from KFC?

A) If

B) Japan

C) Great Britain

96 When will chocolate Santa Clauses be produced?

A) From October

B) Ab August

C) From June

97 In which year did Coca Cola introduce Santa Claus depicted in an advertisement?

A) 1897

B) 1931

C) 1966

98 What was the profession of Jesus' father, Joseph?

A) Carpenter

B) Fisherman

C) Administrator

99 Which archangel visited Mary?

A) Gabriel

B) Michael

C) Raphael

100   What is Santa Claus's zip code in Canada?

A) CLAUS

B) 2512

C) H0H 0H0

101

A)

B)

C)

102

A)

B)

C)

Variant with Quiz Master:

In the version with a quiz master, the reader cannot guess because the answers are marked within the questions.

At the end of the book, there is an overview of all correct solutions at a glance.

Have fun solving it :-)!

1   When was Christmas first celebrated?

➡ A) in the 4th century

B) in the 15th century

C) in the year 3 after Christ

> Christmas was officially celebrated for the first time in the 4th century. The Church designated December 25th to honor the birth of Jesus Christ. This date was also chosen to replace pagan festivals like the Roman "Sol Invictus" (Festival of the Unconquered Sun) with a Christian celebration.

2   How many needles does an average (1.70 m tall) Christmas tree have?

A) 470.000

B) 690.000

➡ C) 180.000

3 Who ordered the census that Mary and Joseph traveled to Bethlehem for?

A) Pontius Pilate

➡ B) Emperor Augustus

C) King Herod

4 What day the British call Boxing Day?

→ A) December 26th

B) December 24th

C) January 6th

5 Where does the term gingerbread come from?

→ A) Probably the mixture of Laib and Libum

B) A sheet cake cut into pieces

C) Jesus received life on earth

6 What is the name of a legendary Christmas dish from Great Britain?

A) Santa Cheese Boots

B) Jelly Bag Cap Cake

→ C) Plum pudding

7 Where does the tradition of Christmas bonuses come from that many employees receive?

A) A tradition in Israel

➤B) From a tradition of the earlier guilds

C) From the toy industry lobby

In these craft organizations, journeymen and apprentices often received an extra payment or gift during the Christmas season. This was a way to honor their work and support them in celebrating the holidays.

8 What is the name of the Grinch's dog in "How the Grinch Stole Christmas"?

➤A) Max

B) Charlie

C) Spike

9 What Christmas beverage is also known as "milk punch"?

➤A) Eggnog

B) Hot Chocolate

C) Mulled Wine

10 What is traditionally hidden inside a Christmas pudding?

A) A key

→B) A coin

C) A candy cane

11 Why do we celebrate Christmas on December 25th?

→A) December 25th has been a religious holiday since 336 AD

B) It is the day of Jesus' birth recorded in the Bible

C) Pope Leo III established it in 801

12 What is a nativity play?

A) An old musical instrument

→B) A play that is performed at Christmas

C) A Christmas board game for the whole family

13 What is special about Finnish Santa Claus Joulupukki?

A) He has no beard

➤ B) He is married

C) He does not have a red coat but one made of reindeer fur

14 According to the biblical Christmas story, which animals witness the birth of Jesus?

A) Ox and donkey

B) Camels

➤ C) None of these

The Bible does not specifically mention animals present at Jesus' birth. However, nativity scenes often depict an ox and a donkey. This comes from ancient traditions and symbolizes the humility of Jesus' birth in a stable.

15 In the song "The Twelve Days of Christmas", what gift is given on the fifth day?

A) Three silver spoons

➤ B) Five golden rings

C) Two turtle doves

16   Who invented the Advent calendar?

A) The Romans around 400 AD

➤B) A German publisher

C) The Chocolate Industry in the 20th Century

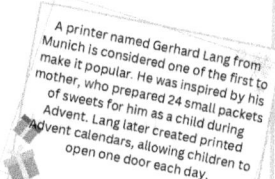

A printer named Gerhard Lang from Munich is considered one of the first to make it popular. He was inspired by his mother, who prepared 24 small packets of sweets for him as a child during Advent. Lang later created printed Advent calendars, allowing children to open one door each day.

17 When does the Christmas season officially end in Germany?

A) On New Year's Eve

B) On December 27th

➤C) On January 6th or on Candlemas in early February

18 In some regions of Germany there are Dambedei, Stutenkerl or Grittibänz. What is that?

➤A) Men made from yeast pastries

B) A carousel with singing

C) A Christmas dwarf who brings the rod to bad children

19 The author of "Lord of the Rings" J. R. R. Tolkien wrote...

A) as a child "Five Little Reindeer"

➤ B) involuntarily the book "Letters from Father Christmas"

C) due to a lost bet the song "Jingle Bells"

20 Who visited Jesus first?

➤ A) The Shepherds

B) The Wise Men of the East

C) King Herod

In the Christmas story from the Bible, an angel appears to shepherds working in the nearby fields. The angel tells them about Jesus' birth and shares the message that the Savior has been born. The shepherds go to see the baby in the manger.

21 Where does the poinsettia plant come from?

A) From the Mohawk of North America

B) From the Aborigines of Australia

➤ C) From the Aztecs of Mexico

22 In Finland, children run before Christmas from house to house. They dress up as...

→A) Elves

B) Reindeer

C) Santa Claus

23 Who distributes the presents in Iceland?

→A) The 13 Yule Lads, called Jólasveinar

B) Santa Claus, called Jólasveinn

C) The 21 volcano elves, called Eldfjallálfar

24 Where did the idea for the song "Rudolph The Red Nose Reindeer" come from?

A) From the eighth American President Martin van Buren

B) The idea comes from composer Johnny Marks

→C) From a children's coloring book

25   In Catalonia, the nativity scene is...

A) a tapa of plums wrapped in bacon as an offering

➤ B) a Catalan Caganer

C) an ivory sledge

26 What famous ballet is often performed around Christmas?

A) Swan Lake

➤ B) The Nutcracker

C) Sleeping Beauty

27   What country started the tradition of sending Christmas cards?

A) Italy

B) France

➤ C) England

28   Where does the Christkind come from?

➤A) Martin Luther introduced it in the 16th century

B) It comes from Christmas traditions in Scandinavia

C) It is an invention of Walt Disney

> The Christkind tradition originates from Martin Luther. Before the Reformation, Saint Nicholas was the central figure of the Christmas season. Luther wanted to shift the focus more toward Jesus Christ and introduced the Christkind.

29   What is marzipan made of?

A) Walnuts

B) Dates

➤C) Almonds

30   According to the Office for Christmas Carols in Graz, approximately how many Christmas carols are there?

➤A) 30.000

B) 3.000

C) 300

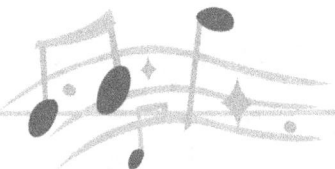

31 What is the origin of the custom to put up a Christmas tree?

A) In Israel, fir trees are exotic lucky charms

→B) This comes from pagan cultures or religions

C) It says so in the Bible

Long before Christianity, people decorated evergreen plants, such as fir branches, during winter.

32 What is Frosty the Snowman's nose made of?

→A) A button

B) A carrot

C) A coal

33 How many candles did the Advent wreath have when it was invented?

→A) 23

B) From the beginning there were 4

C) 1; in rare cases 2

The Advent wreath was invented in 1839 by theologian Johann Hinrich Wichern. He used it in an orphanage in Hamburg to help children count down the days to Christmas. The original wreath had 23 candles: 4 large ones for the Sundays of Advent and 19 smaller ones for the weekdays in between.

34 How many parts of raisins, candied orange peel and candied lemon peel must a raisin stollen contain per 100g of flour?

A) 5g

➤B) 60g

C) 85g

> A raisin stollen must contain at least 60g of raisins, candied orange peel, and candied lemon peel combined per 100g of flour, according to the German guidelines for fine baked goods. This ensures the typical flavor and texture of a traditional stollen. The minimum amount guarantees a certain quality and the characteristic taste.

35 What is the minimum alcohol content of mulled wine in Germany to be called mulled wine?

A) 12%

➤B) 7%

C) There is no regulation for this

> This rule ensures the quality and consistency of the drink; otherwise, it would not be sold as "mulled wine" but classified as a different type of hot beverage.

36 The grandfather of Cedric (Little Lord Fauntleroy) is

A) Earl of Essex

B) Earl of Grantham

➤C) Earl of Dorincort

37 According to a survey, what do Germans give away the most?

➤ A) Vouchers

B) Socks

C) Technology

38 What does the Latin word "adventus" mean?

➤ A) Arrival

B) Almighty

C) candle

39 The Christmas Oratorio tells the Christmas story in 6 cantatas. Who composed it?

A) Ludwig van Beethoven

➤ B) Johann Sebastian Bach

C) Richard Wagner

40 What is the name of the miser in "A Christmas Carol" by Charles Dickens?

A) Baltasar Grooge

B) Dagon Drooge

→ C) Ebenezer Scrooge

41 Which animal do people in Bolivia traditionally bring to Christmas mass?

A) Calf

B) Sheep

→ C) Rooster

42 What was the Christmas tree originally decorated with before baubles and tinsel were used?

→ A) Apples, baked goods and paper

B) Gold and silver jewelry

C) Nuts and oranges

43 What do Catholics call the four Sundays of Advent?

A) Matthew, Mark, Luke and John

B) Lithus, Adventus, Domino und Nubes

→ C) Ad te levavi, Populus Sion, Gaudete und Rorare

44 There is no Santa Claus in Russia, but...

A) Brother Nicolai

→ B) Father Frost

C) Babuschka Sweater

Father Frost, known as "Ded Moroz" in Russian, is a traditional figure who, like Santa Claus, delivers gifts. He is depicted as an older man with a long white beard, usually wearing a blue or red coat.

45 What gifts did the wise men from the East bring for Jesus?

→ A) Gold, frankincense and myrrh

B) Jewelry, nuts and toys

C) Robes, scrolls and salt

46 What are the two other most popular names for Santa Claus?

A) Santa John and Claus Nicholas

B) Father Christmas and Snowman Nick

➤C) Kris Kringle and Saint Nick

47 Which spices should definitely not be used in speculaas?

A) Cardamom and cloves

➤B) Oregano and marjoram

C) Coriander and cinnamon

48 Jesus came to earth to...

A) to heal the sick

B) to take over the government of Israel

➤C) to save lost people from eternal damnation

> Christianity teaches that all humans are separated from God because of their sins, which are mistakes or wrongdoings. This separation leads to eternal damnation, a state of being without God. Jesus, God's Son, came to bridge this gap. He died on the cross to take the punishment for human sins. Those who believe in Him are saved and can live with God.

49 What was the first song ever broadcast from space?

A) Silent Night

→ B) Jingle Bells

C) Deck the Halls

50 Where does the Nordmann fir originally come from?

A) Sweden

→ B) Caucasus

C) Finland

51 What are the names of the other reindeer besides Rudolph?

→ A) Dasher, Dancer, Prancer, Vixen, Comet, Cupid, Donner, Blitzen

B) Glitter, Snowflake, Glory, Starlet, Cupcake and Brownie

C) Unicorn, Lilly, Arnold, Shooting Star und White Mountain

52 In the movie "Home Alone", where are the McCallisters going on vacation when they leave Kevin behind?

➤ A) Paris

B) London

C) Rome

53 Where do gingerbread cookies originally come from?

A) Israel

➤ B) Egypt

C) France

The ancient Egyptians baked a type of honey cake that was offered to their gods. This tradition later spread to Europe, where the honey cake was refined and eventually became what we know today as gingerbread.

54 Since when have electric Christmas tree lights been around?

A) 1879, with the invention of the light bulb

B) 1911, a department store chain in Berlin launches it

➤ C) Invented in 1882, used in the White House in 1895

55 What color was Santa Claus' coat, before Coca Cola dressed him in red?

→ A) Blue

B) Gold

C) White

56 Traditionally, many families in Australia and New Zealand celebrate Christmas on the beach, with...

A) the election of the most beautiful Santa Claus (Mr. Santa)

→ B) a big barbecue, called BBQ in English

C) a surfing competition on red and white boards

57 What do many people in Poland hang on the Christmas tree?

→ A) Spiders and spider webs

B) Wool socks

C) Small wooden dolls

58 In which city was Saint Nicholas bishop?

→ A) Myra

B) Jerusalem

C) Corinthians

59 How many kilos does the average German gain between December 1st and New Year's Day?

A) 1-2

→ B) 3-5

C) 5-7

60 According to the biblical story, where was Jesus born?

→ A) Bethlehem

B) Jerusalem

C) Nazareth

61 In the song "Rudolph the Red-Nosed Reindeer", what was Rudolph not allowed to do?

A) Fly Santa's sleigh

B) Go to the North Pole

➤ C) Join in any reindeer games

62 What is the highest-grossing Christmas movie of all time?

A) Elf

B) The Polar Express

➤ C) Home Alone

63 In "The Polar Express", what is the first gift of Christmas?

➤ A) A silver bell from Santa's sleigh

B) A golden ticket

C) A mystery snow globe

64 Which islands do not exist?

→ A) Advent Islands

B) Christmas Island

C) Easter Island

65 When are the presents distributed in Spain?

→ A) January 6

B) December 25th

C) February 2nd

66 Where do traditional Christmas pyramids come from?

A) From Mexico

→ B) From the German Ore Mountains

C) From Kazakh farmers

Christmas pyramids traditionally come from the Erzgebirge (Ore Mountains) in Germany. This region is famous for its woodcraft. In the past, when mining was the main job, people looked for other income during the winter. They started making wooden art.

67 Why is the birth of Jesus something absolutely unique and special?

A) No human being was ever laid in a manger

B) Shepherds worshiped Jesus

➤ C) God himself took human form

In Jesus Christ, God Himself entered the world to restore the relationship between God and humanity, which had been broken by sin. This demonstrates God's profound love and His willingness to be close to humanity and bring salvation.

68 On which album was the 1986 song "Last Christmas" by Wham! released?

➤ A) Music from The Edge Of Heaven

B) Make it Big

C) Fantastic

69 Has the celebration of Christmas ever been banned?

A) Yes, in Brazil from 1963 to 1971

➤ B) Yes, between 1647 and 1660 in England

C) No

70 Which event takes place every year at Christmas in Rio de Janeiro: Santa Claus...

→ A) lands in the football stadium with a helicopter

B) gives a speech on Rede Globo, a major TV channel

C) distributes candy to children in need

71 Why is tinsel called tinsel?

A) Llamas in South America were decorated with silver threads

B) The inventor was called Lambrecht Etta

→ C) It comes from Italian and means metal leaf

72 Continue: And the angel said unto them, "Fear not, for behold, I bring you good tidings...

A) news that will change Israel."

→ B) of great joy, which shall be to all people."

C) secrets that no one else can hear."

73 What do girls in Sweden traditionally wear at Christmas?

A) Santa Claus coats and fake beards

➤ B) White robes and candles on the head

C) Fur hats and velvet gloves

74 Where is the Christmas story?

A) In the letters of Paul

B) In the Psalms

➤ C) In the Gospels

75 What song did the angels sing?

➤ A) Glory to God in the highest

B) Silent Night, Holy Night

C) Oh, how happy you are

76 What does the X in the abbreviation stand for in English X-mas for Christmas?

→A) From the Greek letter Chi

B) This comes from youth language

C) The X stands for the cross on which Christ died

77 Which Asian country is the only one where Christmas is a public holiday?

A) China

→B) South Korea

C) Malaysia

78 Which statement is not true? Speculatius...

→A) must not contain almonds

B) was initially only illustrated with the story of St. Nicholas

C) is eaten all year round in Indonesia

79   Who showed the wise men the way to Jesus?

A) The Angel

B) King Herod

→ C) The Star

80   What does the name "Jesus" mean?

→ A) God saves

B) The Sacrificial One

C) God came as a human

81   What does "Christ" mean?

→ A) The Anointed One

B) The Savior

C) King

82   How does the Christmas story begin?

A) Once upon a time...

B) And so it is told...

C) And it came to pass in those days...

83   How did the Christmas markets develop?

A) The monks in the monasteries sold their goods

B) Late medieval winter markets for the population

C) It was the idea of clever merchants around 1840

84   What are incense cones made of?

A) Made from resin, charcoal and wood flour

B) From rapeseed oil and gypsum

C) From ground horse hooves

85 What U.S. state was the first to recognize Christmas as an official holiday?

→ A) Alabama

B) New York

C) Texas

86 The star singers write on the doors C+M+B. What does this mean?

A) Christ, Mary, Bethlehem

B) ChristMas beginns

→ C) Christus mansionem benedicat (Christ bless this house)

87 Where did Mary, Joseph and Jesus flee?

A) Lebanon

→ B) Egypt

C) Türkiye

88   Does the Bible say that Jesus was born in a stable?

A) Yes

➤B) No

C) Instead, the word "shed" is

> The Bible mentions in Luke 2:7 that Mary laid Jesus in a manger because there was no room in the inn. The word "stable" is not specifically mentioned, but the manger suggests that it was a place for animals. Over time, the idea of a stable became popular, even though the Bible does not provide exact details.

89   What is myrrh?

A) Beautiful jewelry

B) Children's toys

➤C) Fragrant resin

90   Why is Jesus often called "Jesus of Nazareth"?

A) He was crucified there

B) It was his earthly surname

➤C) He spent his childhood there

91   Who was related to Jesus?

A) Peter

→B) John the Baptist

C) Luke

John the Baptist was a relative of Jesus. Their mothers, Mary and Elizabeth, were cousins. The Bible says John was born before Jesus and had the mission to prepare the way for Him. He baptized people and preached about the coming of the Messiah.

92   What does "Merry Christmas" mean in Spanish?

A) Muchas Gracias

→B) Feliz Navidad

C) Bienvenidos

93 Why do some people in America hang cucumbers on their Christmas tree?

→A) People think cucumbers bring good luck

B) Cucumbers are part of every Christmas meal

C) The smell of cucumbers creates a great atmosphere

94   Which Christmas film features Tom Hanks 6 Characters?

A) Snow Queen

B) Charlie and the Chocolate Factory

→ C) The Polar Express

95 In which country is Christmas dinner ordered from KFC?

A) If

→ B) Japan

C) Great Britain

This started in the 1970s with a smart marketing campaign promoting "Kentucky for Christmas." Since Japan doesn't have a traditional Christmas meal, KFC became a popular substitute. Today, it's a cherished tradition, with people queuing up and placing orders well in advance.

96   When will chocolate Santa Clauses be produced?

A) From October

B) Ab August

→ C) From June

97 In which year did Coca Cola introduce Santa Claus depicted in an advertisement?

A) 1897

➤ B) 1931

C) 1966

98 What was the profession of Jesus' father, Joseph?

➤ A) Carpenter

B) Fisherman

C) Administrator

99 Which archangel visited Mary?

➤ A) Gabriel

B) Michael

C) Raphael

100

What is Santa Claus's zip code in Canada?

A) CLAUS

B) 2512

➤ C) H0H 0H0

This special postal code was created by Canada Post to allow children to send letters to Santa. The mix of letters and numbers looks like Santa's classic "Ho Ho Ho" and is a fun way to bring holiday cheer to children.

101

A)

B)

C)

102

A)

B)

C)

solutions

#	Ans	#	Ans	#	Ans	#	Ans	#	Ans
01	A	21	C	41	C	61	C	81	A
02	C	22	A	42	A	62	C	82	C
03	B	23	A	43	C	63	A	83	B
04	A	24	C	44	B	64	A	84	A
05	A	25	B	45	A	65	A	85	A
06	C	26	B	46	C	66	B	86	C
07	B	27	C	47	B	67	C	87	B
08	A	28	A	48	C	68	A	88	B
09	A	29	C	49	B	69	B	89	C
10	B	30	A	50	B	70	A	90	C
11	A	31	B	51	A	71	C	91	B
12	B	32	A	52	A	72	B	92	B
13	B	33	A	53	B	73	B	93	A
14	C	34	B	54	C	74	C	94	C
15	B	35	B	55	A	75	A	95	B
16	B	36	C	56	B	76	A	96	C
17	C	37	A	57	A	77	B	97	B
18	A	38	A	58	A	78	A	98	A
19	B	39	B	59	B	79	C	99	A
20	A	40	C	60	A	80	A	100	C

Copyright © 2024 Dennis Streichert

Dennis Streichert, Brahmsallee 19, 20144 Hamburg
mail@dennis-streichert.de - https://dennis-streichert.de

All rights reserved.

The work, including its parts, is protected by copyright. Any use outside the narrow limits of copyright law is prohibited without the consent of the publisher and the author. This applies in particular to electronic or other reproduction, translation, distribution and making available to the public.

ISBN-13: 978-3-98880-009-1

www.ingramcontent.com/pod-product-compliance
Lightning Source LLC
LaVergne TN
LVHW020433080526
838202LV00055B/5169